John Seed

Artist's Statements
of the Old Masters

The artist's statements contained in this book were all written by me, with one notable exception. I wrote them by asking myself the following hypothetical question:

"If the great European artists of the past were alive today, what kinds of statements would they need to write to explain and justify their work?"

John Seed

Artists

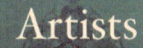

Leonardo da Vinci

Jan Van Eyck

Jean Baptiste Greuze

Diego Velázquez

Hieronymus Bosch

Jean-Honore Fragonard

Titian

Peter Paul Rubens

Frans Hals

Raphael

Jean-Baptiste Greuze

Rachel Ruysch

Juan Sánchez Cotán

Pieter Aertsen

Pieter Claesz

Michelangelo Buonarroti

Jean-Antoine Watteau

Van Dyck

Jusepe de Ribera

Jacques Louis David

Joachim Patinir

Jacob Van Ruisdael

Rembrandt Van Rijn

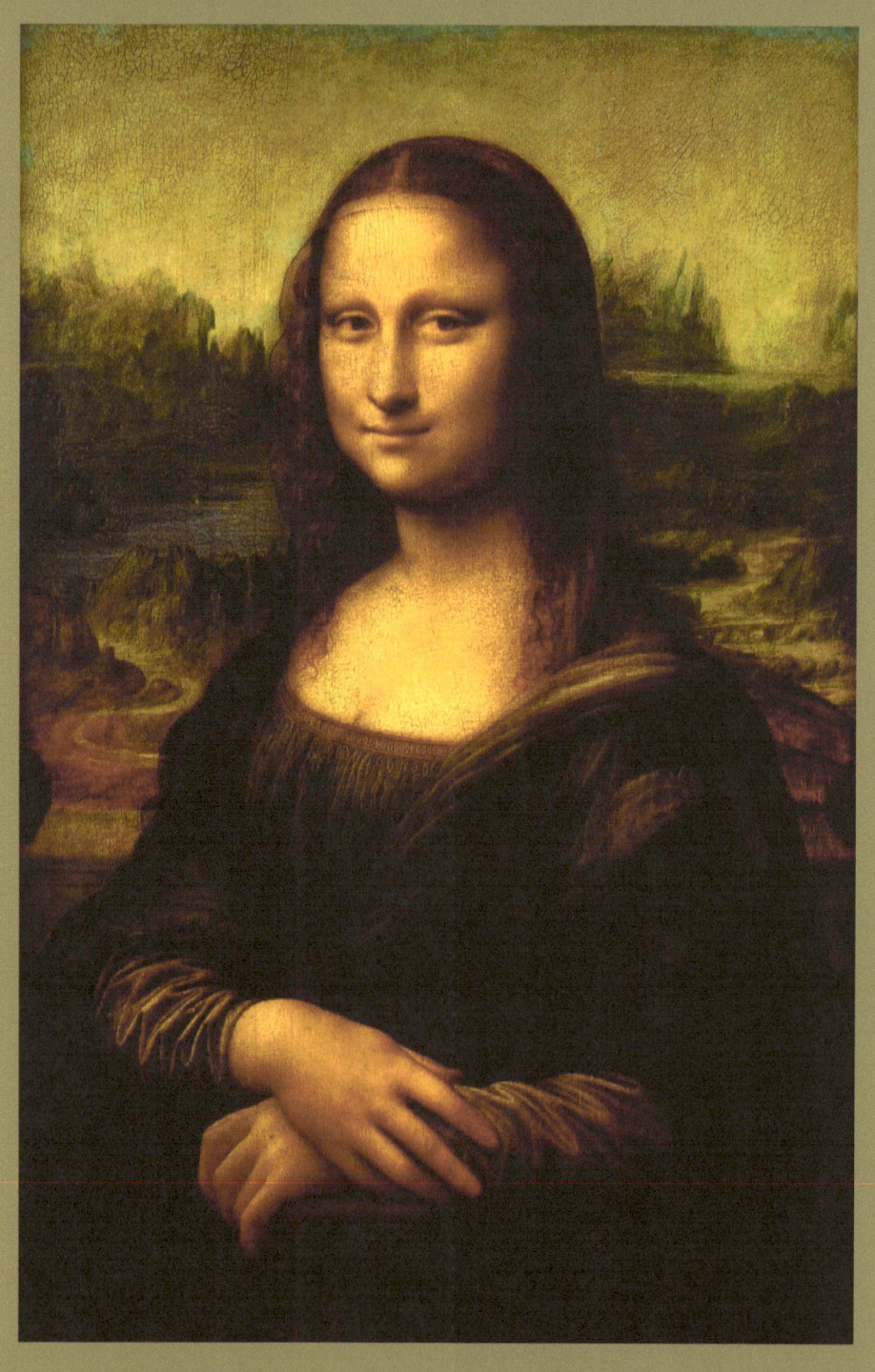

Leonardo da Vinci
La Giaconda (Mona Lisa)
1503-4
The Louvre, Paris

"I originally proposed *La Giaconda* as non-specific vehicle to map coded and opposing systems of selfhood and gender that could be substantiated via an intertextual nexus. Through a personal discursive process, it then evolved towards a self-referential "otherness" that overlays Neo-Platonic androgyny re-defined as an ontology of the unsaid."

— Leonardo da Vinci

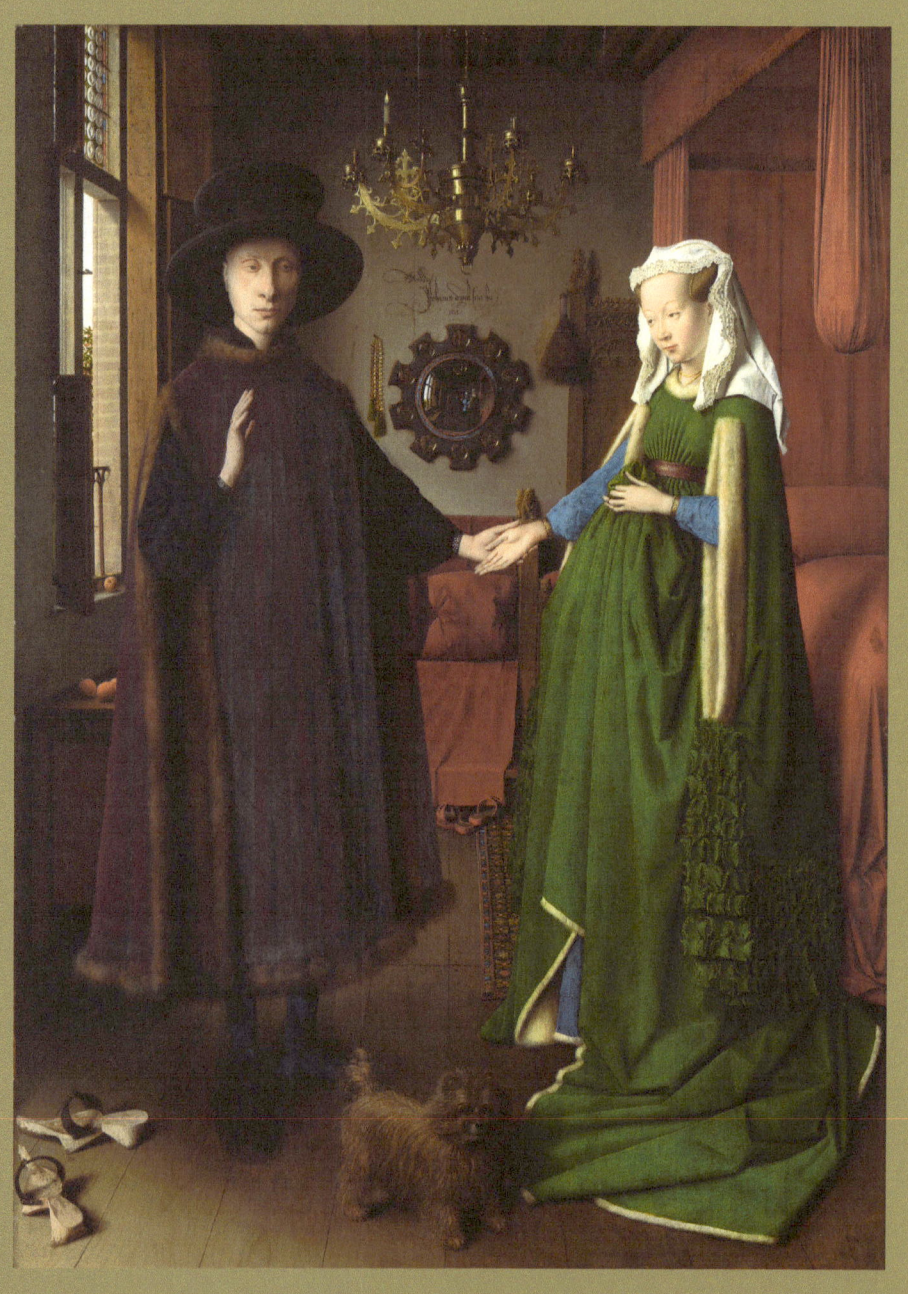

Jan Van Eyck
The Arnolfini Portrait
1434
The National Gallery, London

"This work is a quasi-motivated trichotomy that deconstructs icons, indexes and symbols in a synchronicity activated by 15th century Brugeian mercantilism. By depicting the simultaneity of the bride and groom's dual proprioconceptions I address the implied proto-capitalism motivating their union, interconnecting it with a haptic inaccessibility that in itself constructs a peripheral emotional stasis."

— *Jan Van Eyck*

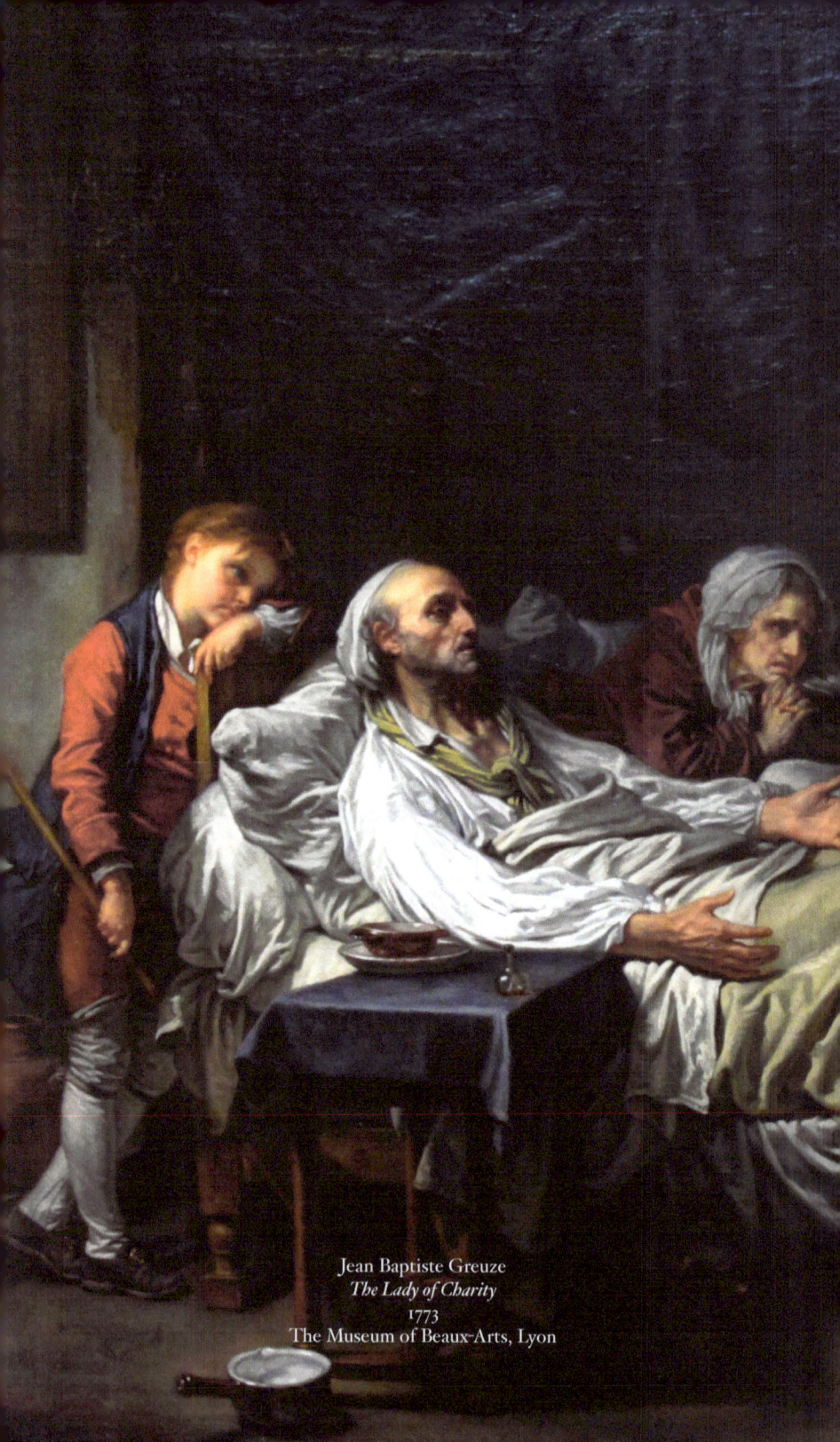

Jean Baptiste Greuze
The Lady of Charity
1773
The Museum of Beaux-Arts, Lyon

"I am interested in subject/object complicity and also in the covert subversion of moral candor. Hence, the obvious voiding and redaction of neutrality that both subjugates and enhances the obvious thematic reductivism of my genre pieces. This then, is the primary tension of my work."

— *Jean Baptiste Greuze*

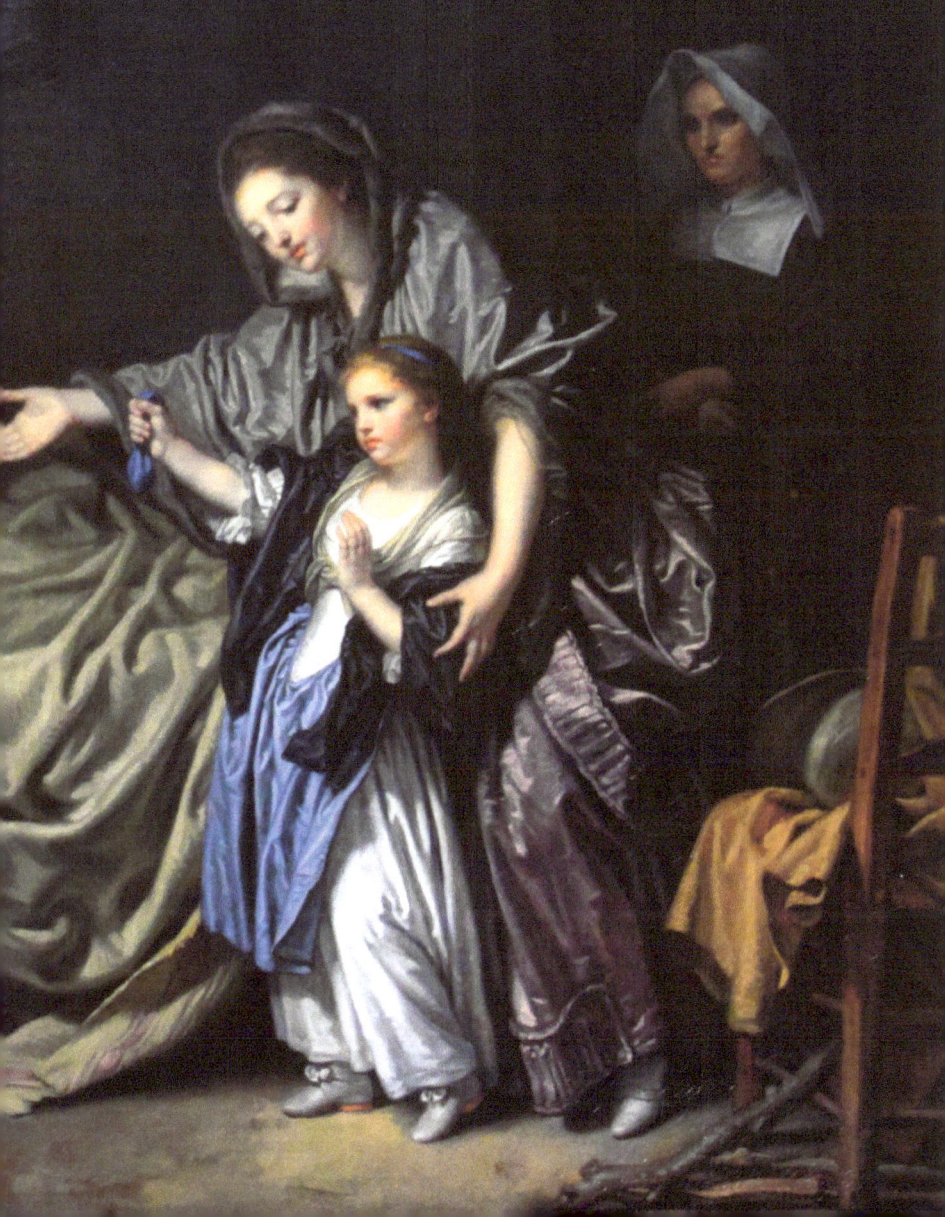

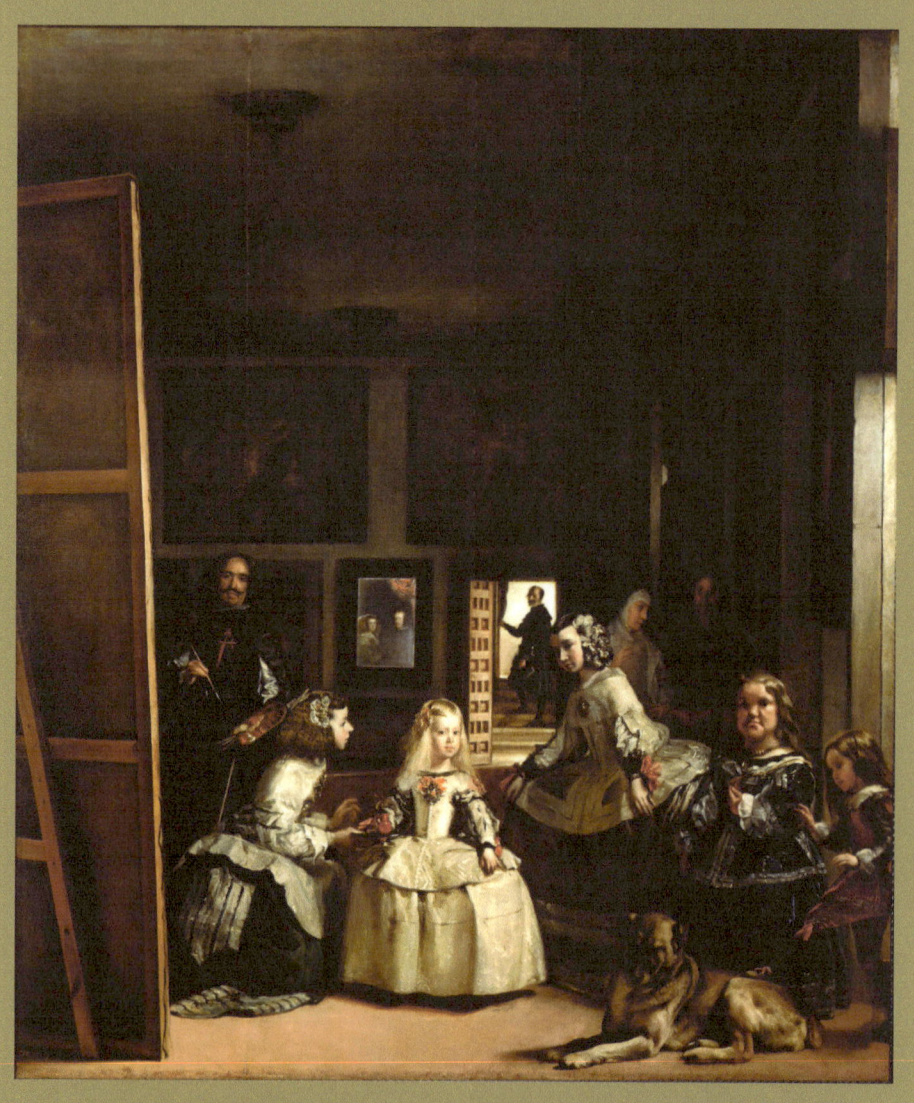

Diego Velázquez
Las Meninas
1639
The Prado, Madrid

"In addressing the collapse of personal autonomy and identity in an authoritarian and monarchist space I imply a multiplicity of didactic constructions and formations. By investigating the formal and informal withdrawal of the central and objective role of the "subject" I address and investigate the role of signifiers and their ontological suggestions. I also reverse and subjugate the traditional symbol of the dog—Fido—into a subject object reflection of the hierarchical and appropriated role of the artist in a Catholic/Baroque social construct."

— *Diego Rodríguez de Silva y Velázquez*

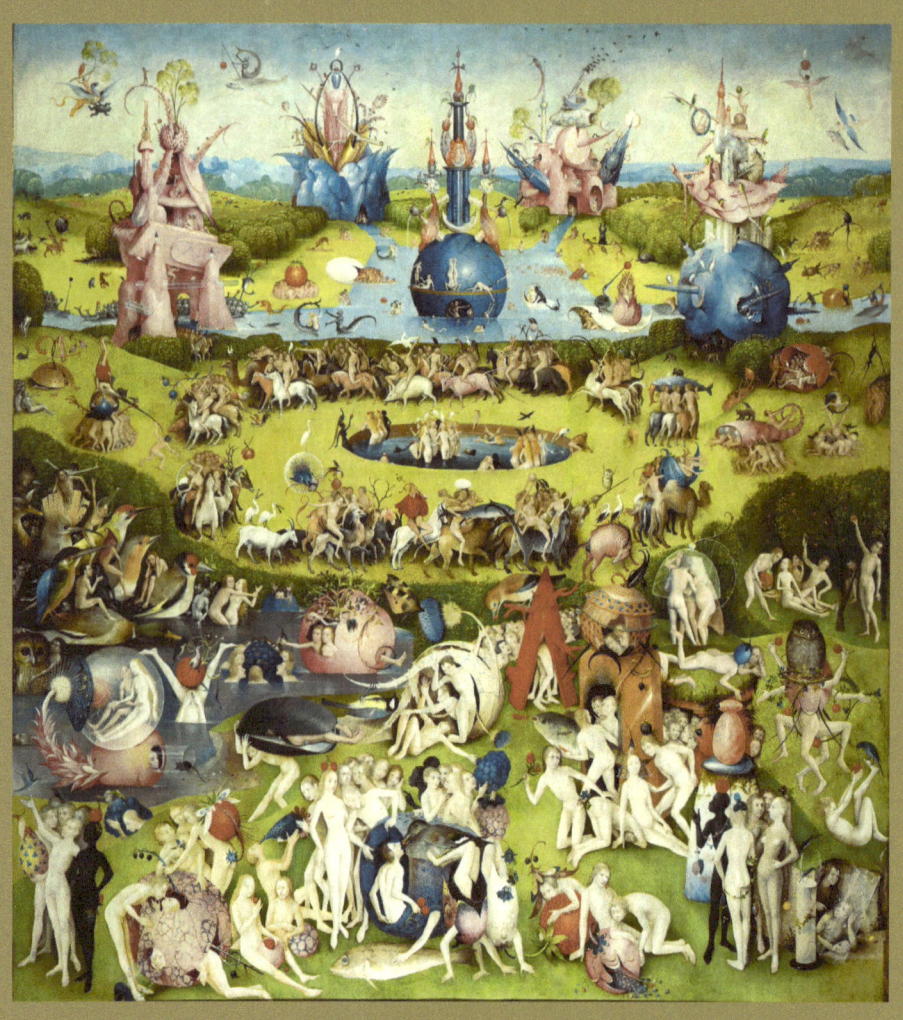

"An implied quasi-theatrical sublimity in my work creates a tension between modes of engagement with internal and external realities. While attempting to bridge a rift in the continuum between metaphysics and narrativity I investigate a lexicon of parafictional erotic proclivities."

— *Hieronymus Bosch*

Hieronymus Bosch
The Garden of Earthly Delights
c.1500
The Prado, Madrid

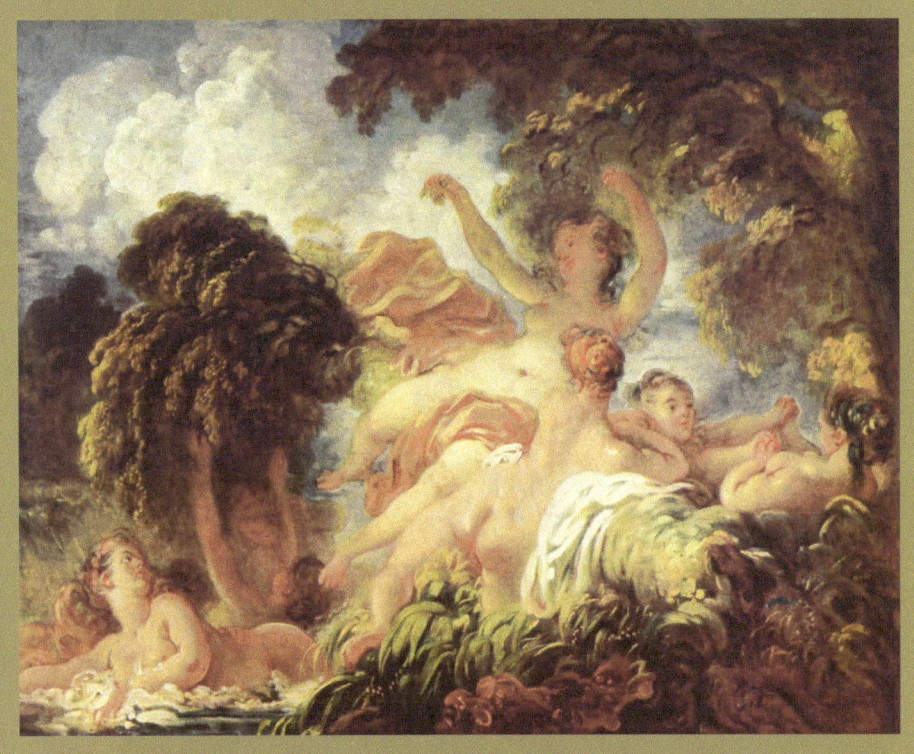

"By disrupting the implied heteronormative discourse of antediluvian mythology, my paintings imply a personal mythopoeic narrative that both transcends and embodies the male gaze. By investigating the callipygian forms of a complex homosocial nexus in an anti-Lacanian context I depict a multitude of redundant, overlapping and coded tasks and roles."

— *Jean-Honore Fragonard*

Jean-Honore Fragonard
The Bathers
c. 1765
The Louvre, Paris

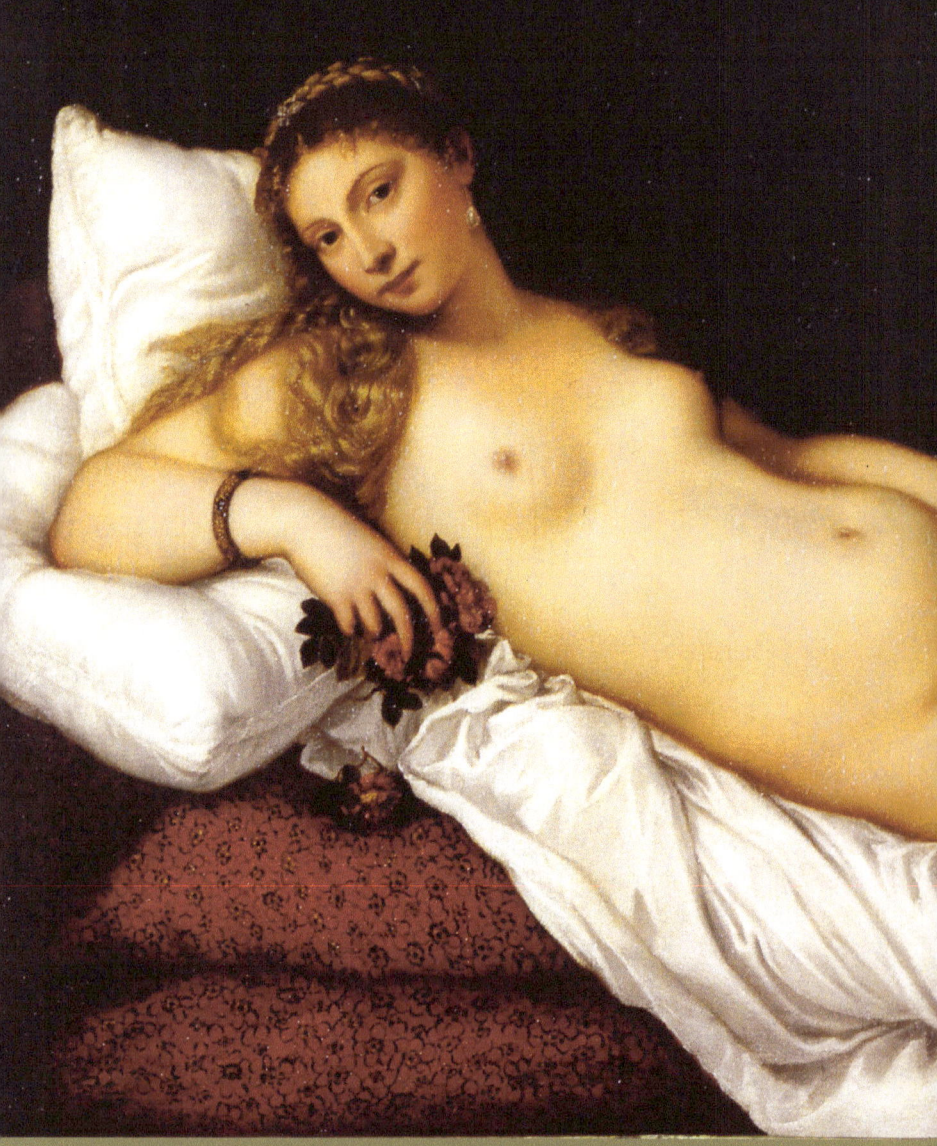

"Woman, goddess, subject, and object: Venus activates both the utopian and dystopian spaces of the Venetian Palazzo. Inducing an affirmative valence of feminine/objective lucidity Venus poses a question: has our tendency to privatize desire further affirmed or disenfranchised her archetypal significance?"

— *Tiziano Vecellio*

Titian
The Venus of Urbino
1538
The Uffizi Gallery, Florence

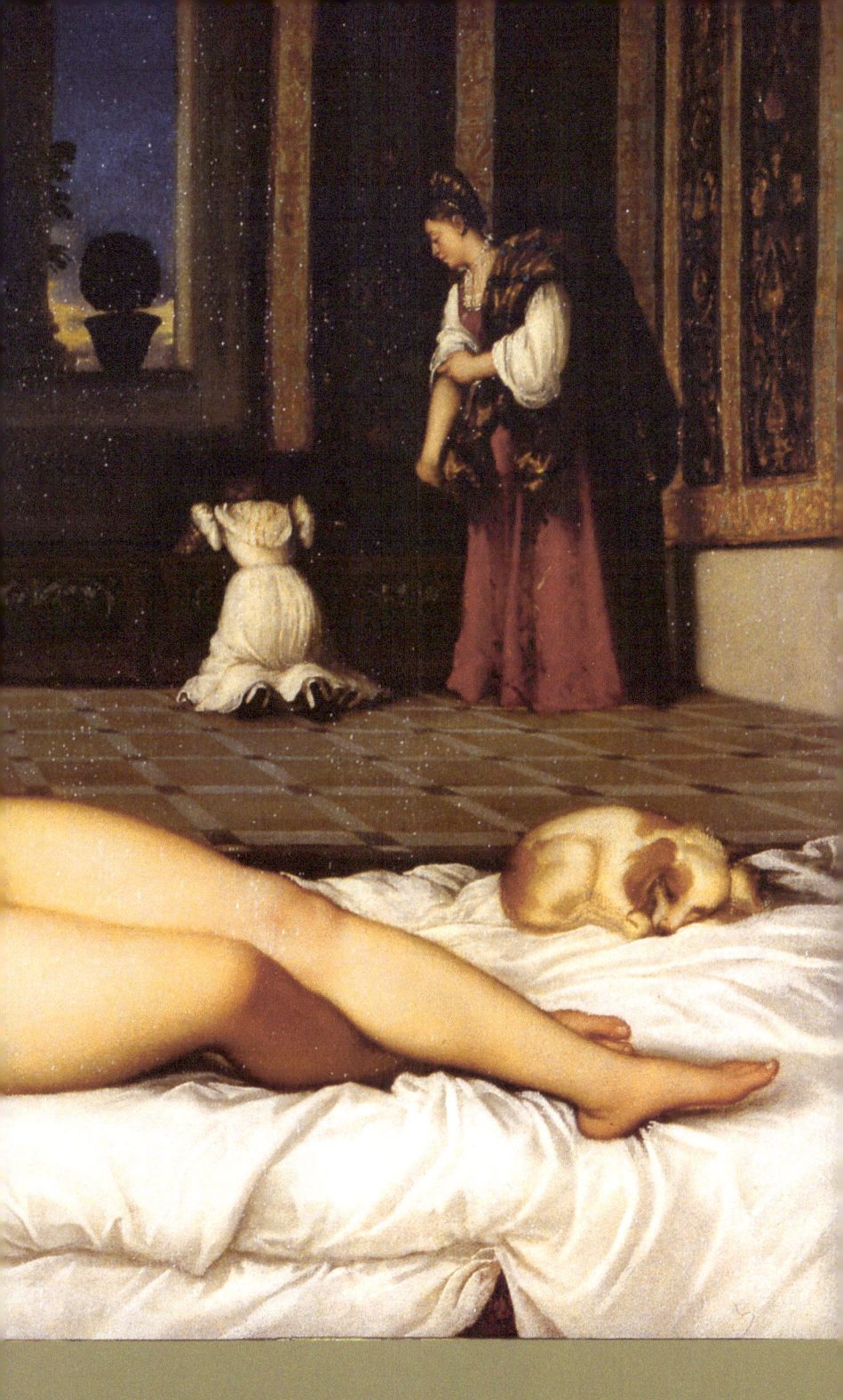

John Seed *Artist's Statements of the Old Masters*

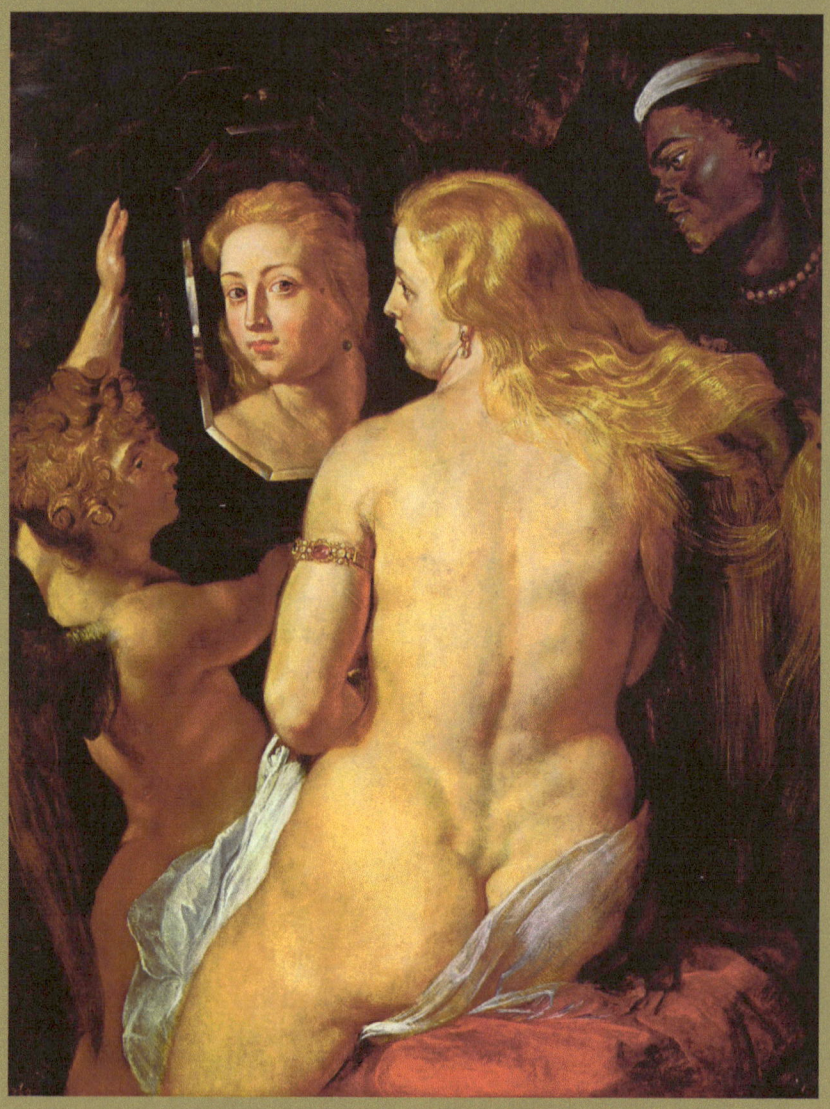

"This painting situates Venus as a multivalent symbol of promiscuity and body dysmorphia. It also deconstructs her whiteness in relation to the figure of a dark-skinned maid, and critiques the subservience of Cupid. It is from a series of works that explore and reconstitute the myth of Venus in a framework of logocentric epistemology designed to refute and re-schematize its previously assumed Eurocentric eroticism."

— *Peter Paul Rubens*

Peter Paul Rubens
Venus in Front of the Mirror
1614-5
Liechtenstein, The Princely Collections

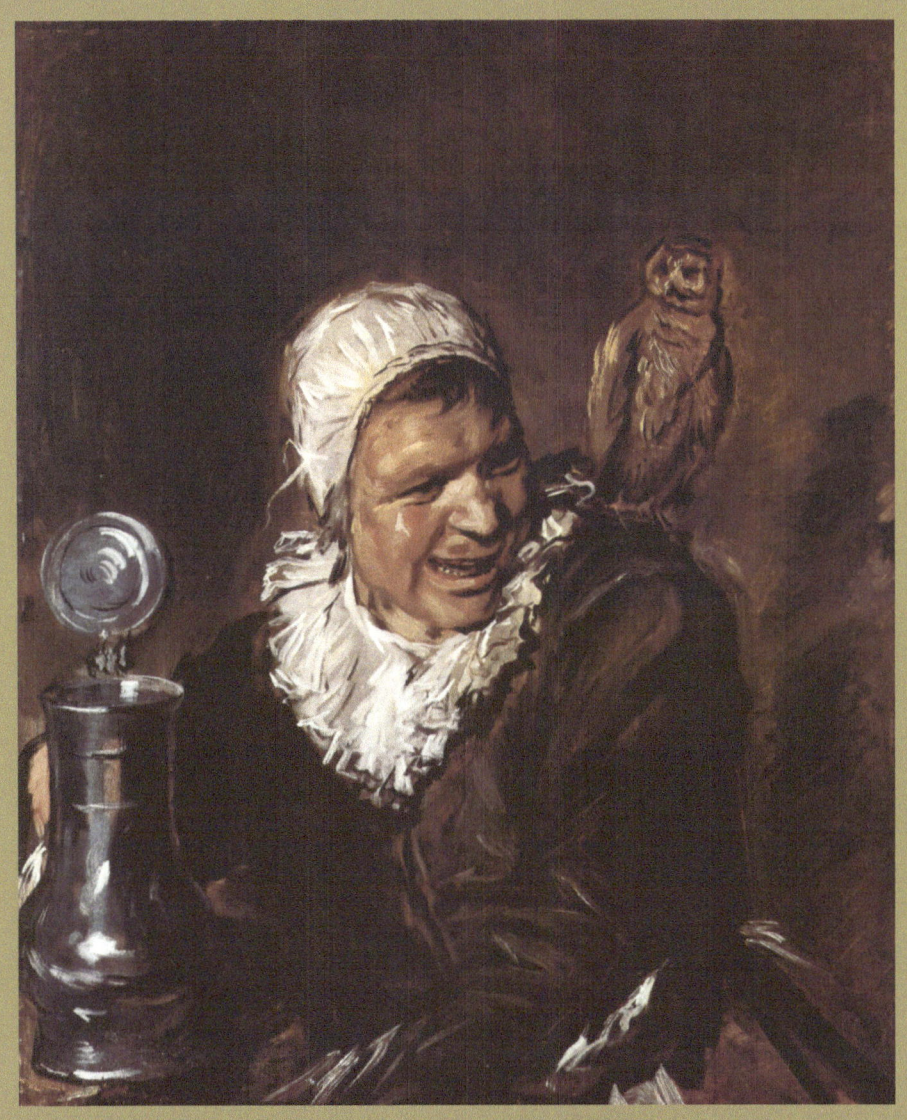

"My interest is in the surveillance of criminality and in the individuation of the marginalized. My portrait *Malle Babbe* is both an essentialist schematization and a personification of the body-organism reconstituted outside of the framework of disciplinary normalization."

— *Frans Hals*

Frans Hals
Malle Babbe (The Witch of Haarlem)
c. 1633-5
Gemäldegalerie, Berlin

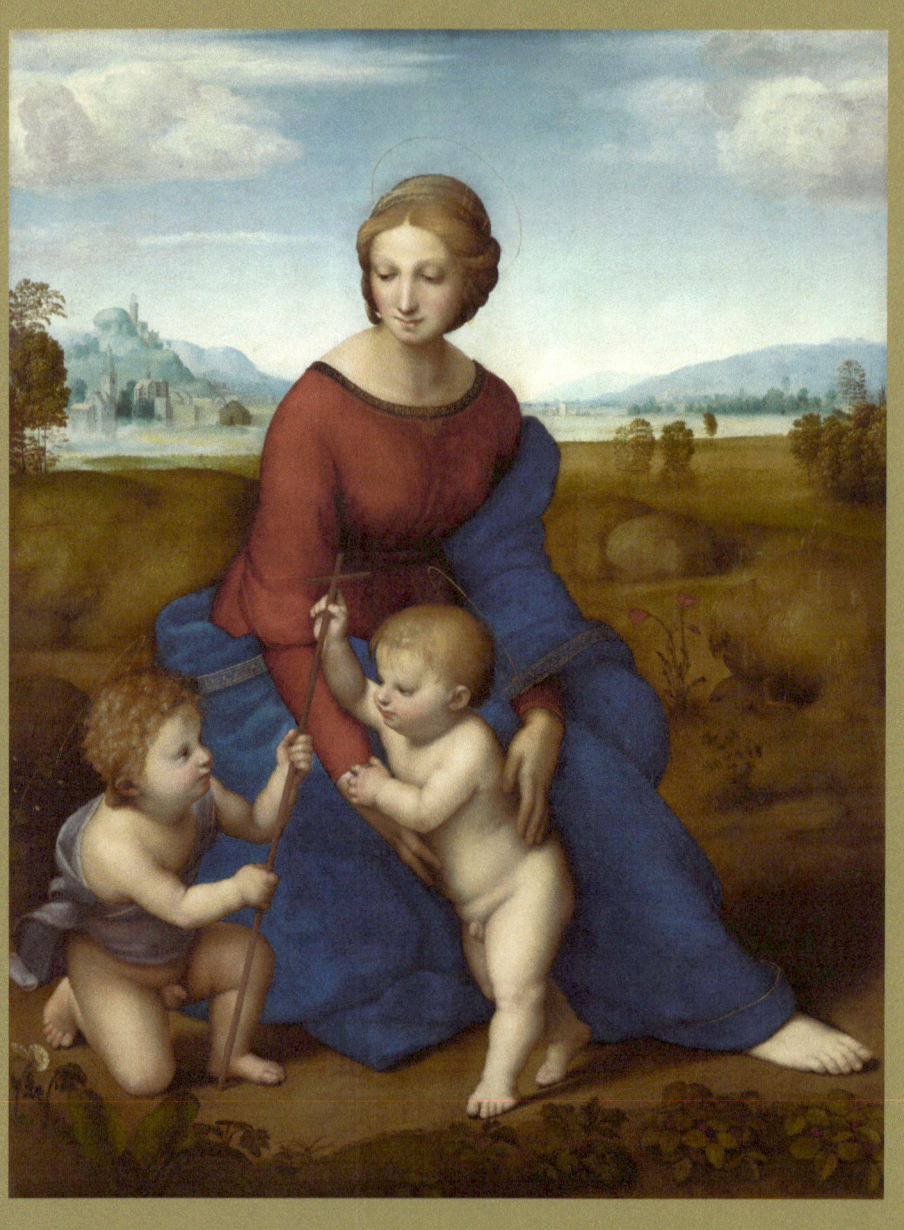

Raphael
Madonna in the Meadow
1505
Kunsthistorisches Museum, Vienna

"*Madonna in the Meadow* is essentially a site of negated conflict composed of ostensibly related forms and items. Its atavistic interchanges of formal elements and inertly referenced mythologized religious events subjugate and transpose its inherent experienceability."

— *Raffaello Sanzio*

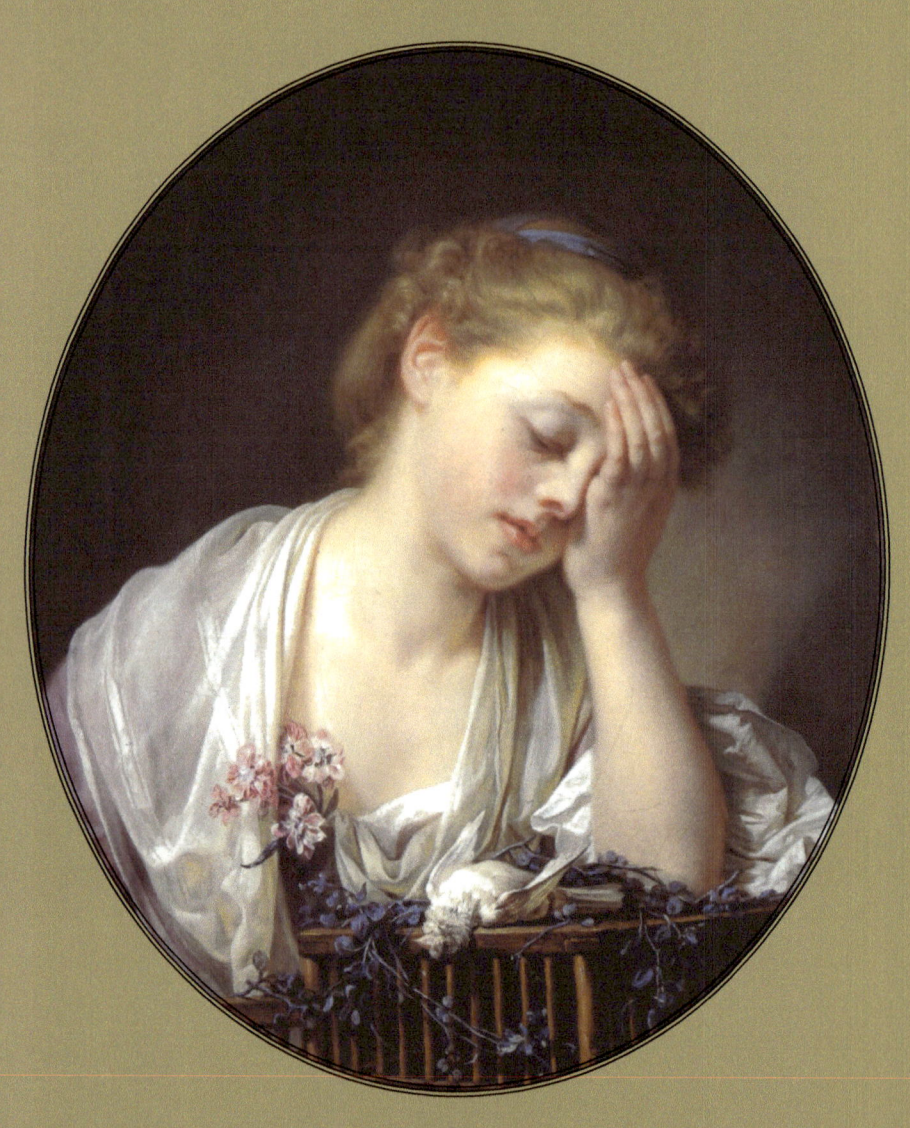

Jean-Baptiste Greuze
Young Girl Crying over her Dead Bird
1765
National Galleries of Scotland, Edinburgh

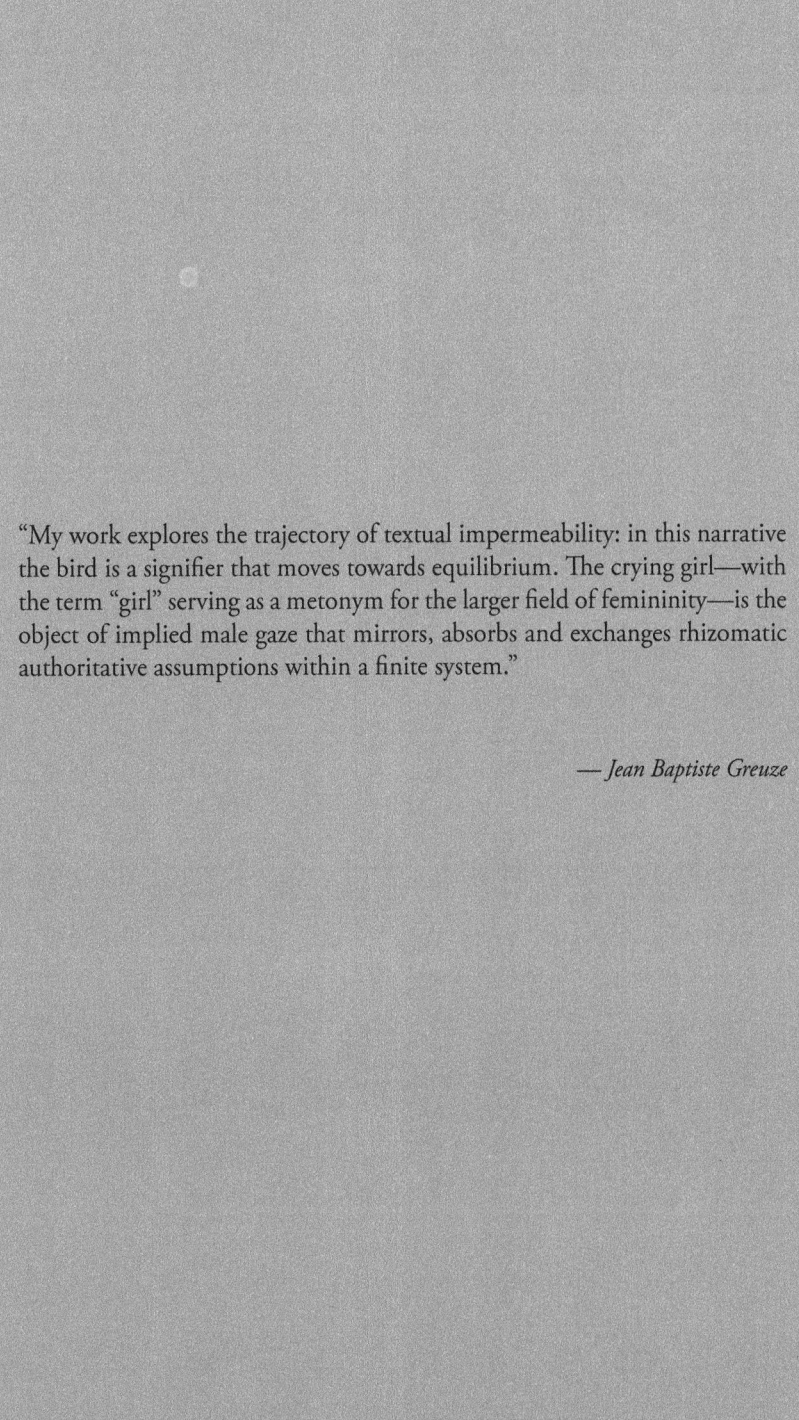

"My work explores the trajectory of textual impermeability: in this narrative the bird is a signifier that moves towards equilibrium. The crying girl—with the term "girl" serving as a metonym for the larger field of femininity—is the object of implied male gaze that mirrors, absorbs and exchanges rhizomatic authoritative assumptions within a finite system."

—— *Jean Baptiste Greuze*

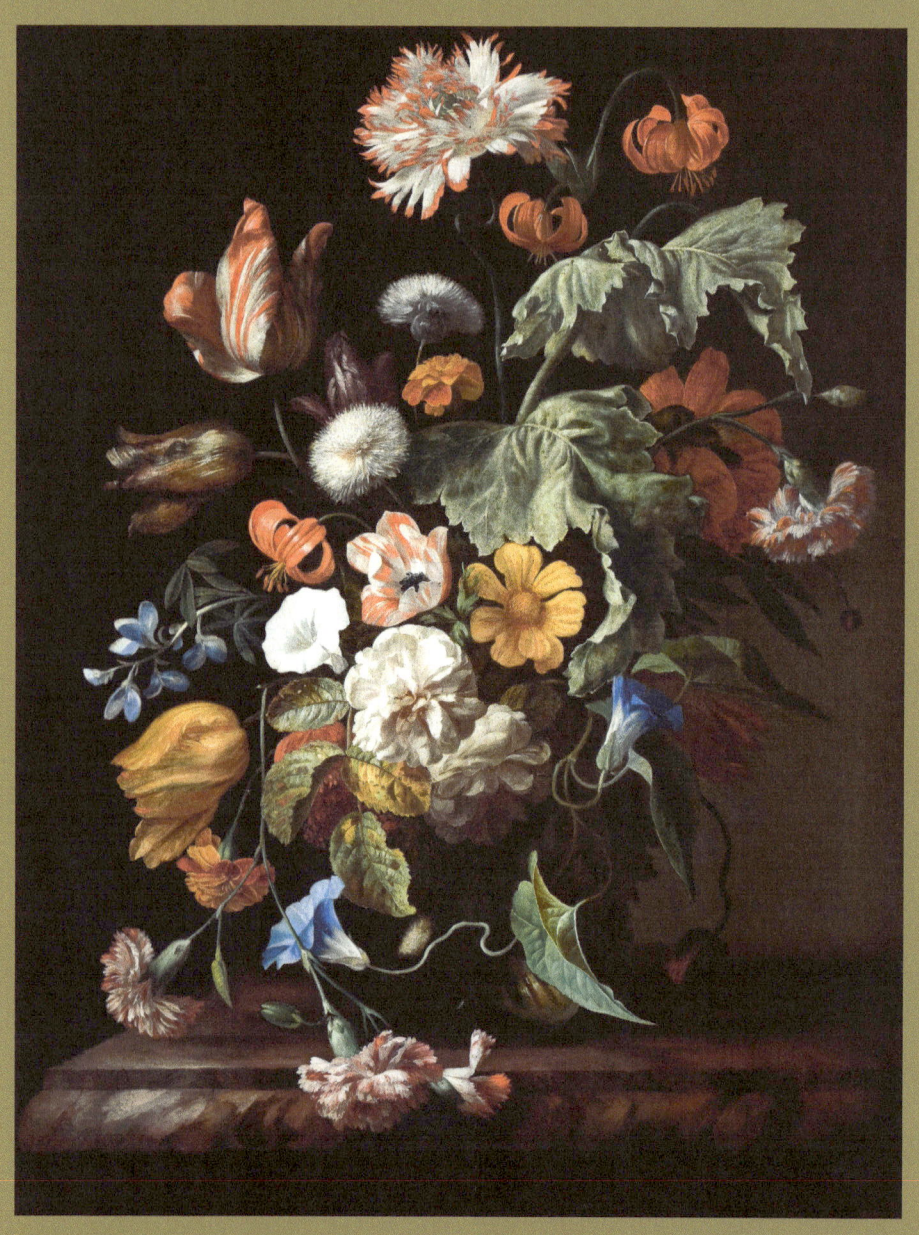

Rachel Ruysch
Still Life with Flowers
c. 1685
The Hallwyl Museum, Stockholm

"*Still Life with Flowers* represents a personal generative model and also a system of arborescent mutualism. The genetic contiguity of the various flowers establishes a familial grouping of synedoches that are both micro and macrocosmic. My goal is to assert and maintain a system of autochthonous hybridity."

— *Rachel Ruysch*

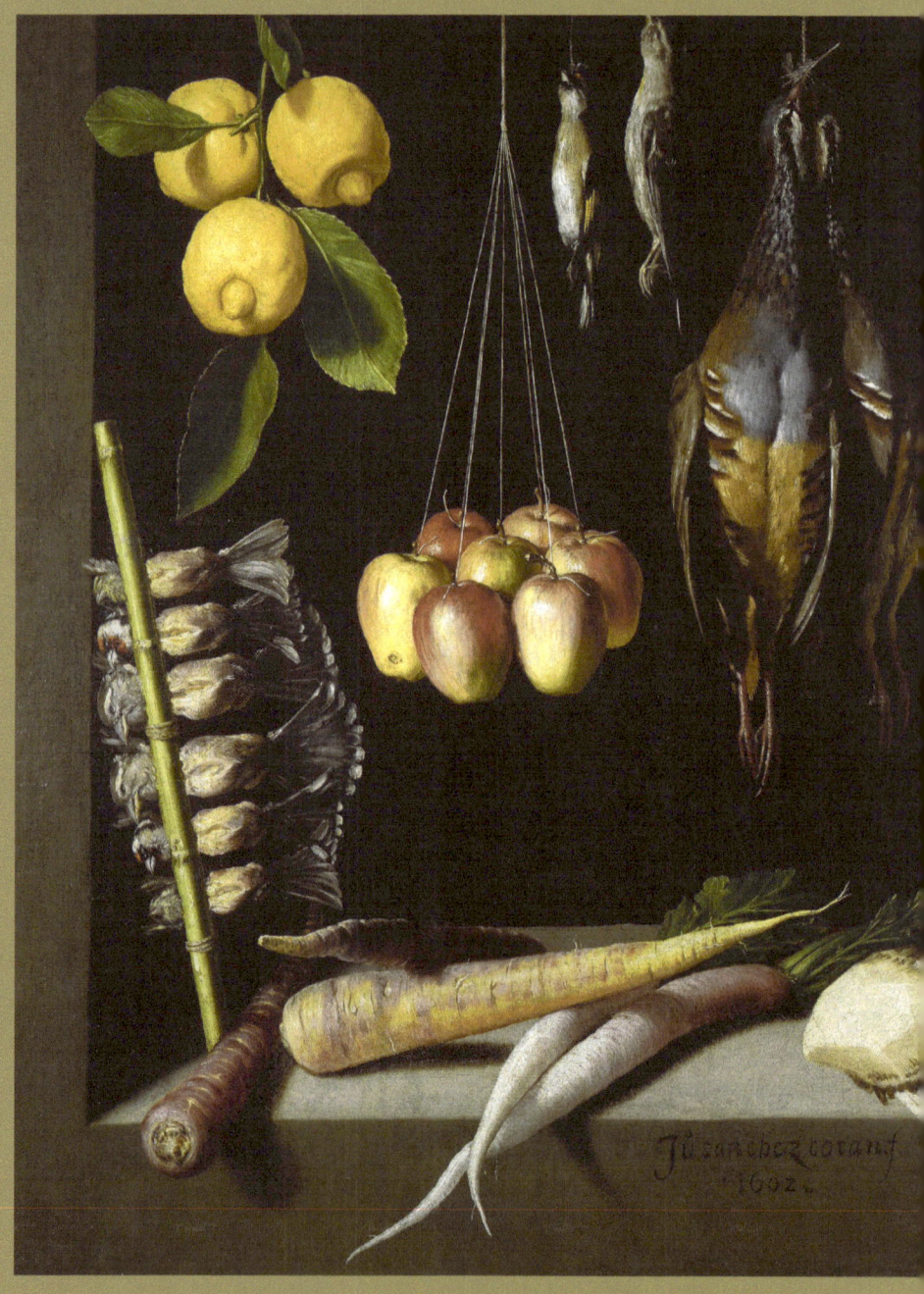

Juan Sánchez Cotán
Still Life with Game Fowl, Vegetables and Fruits
1602
The Prado, Madrid

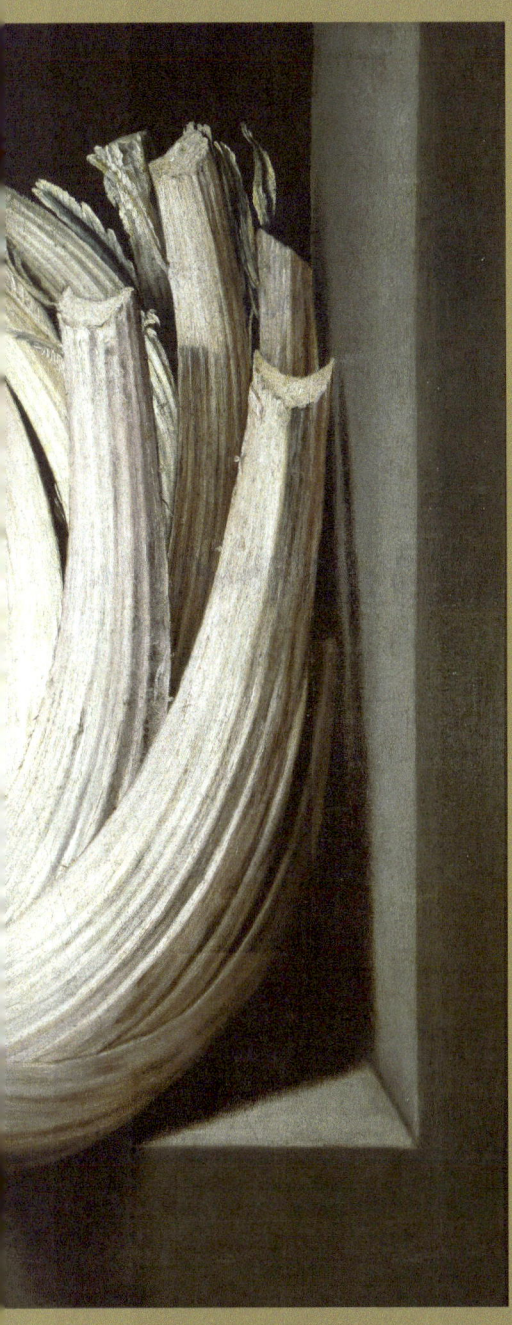

"My work explores the temporal duality of objects/non-objects in a hegemonic space/non-space. Indeed: my fruit, fowl and vegetable simulacra juxtaposes pre-Marxist male/female homo/hetero-social redactions of materiality through recurring formal concerns."

— *Juan Sánchez Cotán*

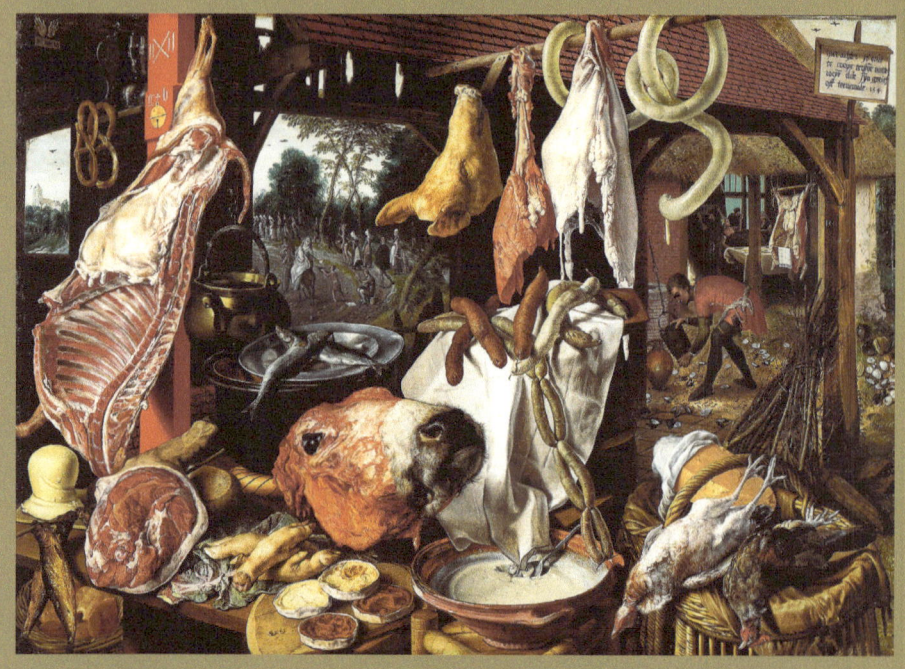

"By deconstructing the sybaritic carnality of a mid-sixteenth century abattoir in relation to its amorphous bio-diversity, I imply a fragmentation of consensus. My canvas narrates and generates a matrix of crypto-normativist trauma that is, in fact, the implicit endpoint of Post-Reformation Catholic metaphysical prurience."

— *Pieter Aertsen*

Pieter Aertsen
Butcher's Stall with the Flight into Egypt
1551
University Art Collections, Uppsala University, Sweden

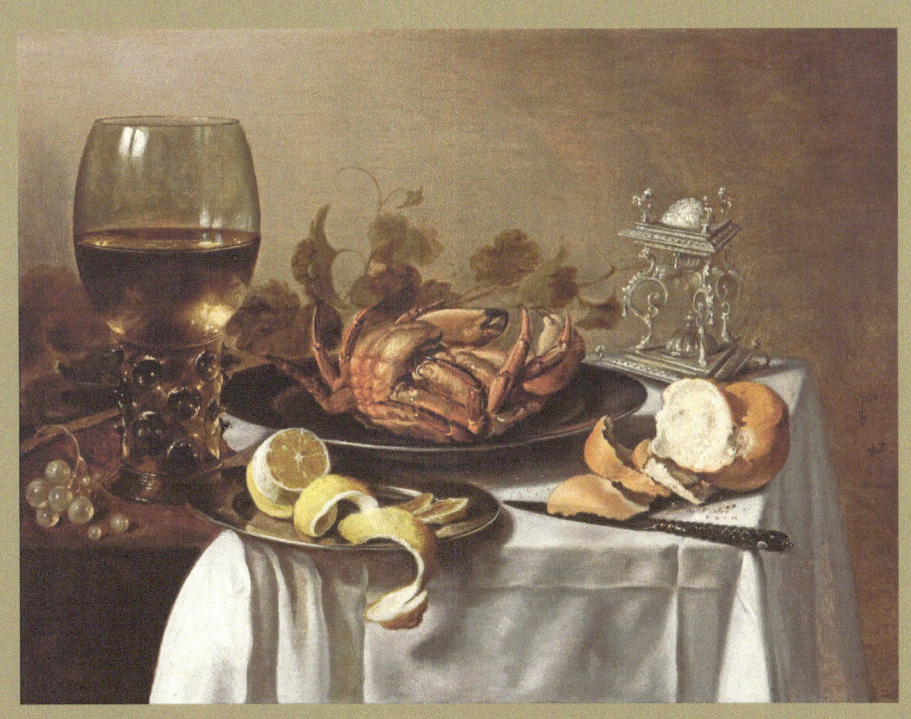

"My still lifes explore the paradoxical fragmentation of attention that accompanies the abnegation of absolute formations. Each object intentionally generates a syntax of anecdotal formations that preferentially resist exegesis."

— *Pieter Claesz*

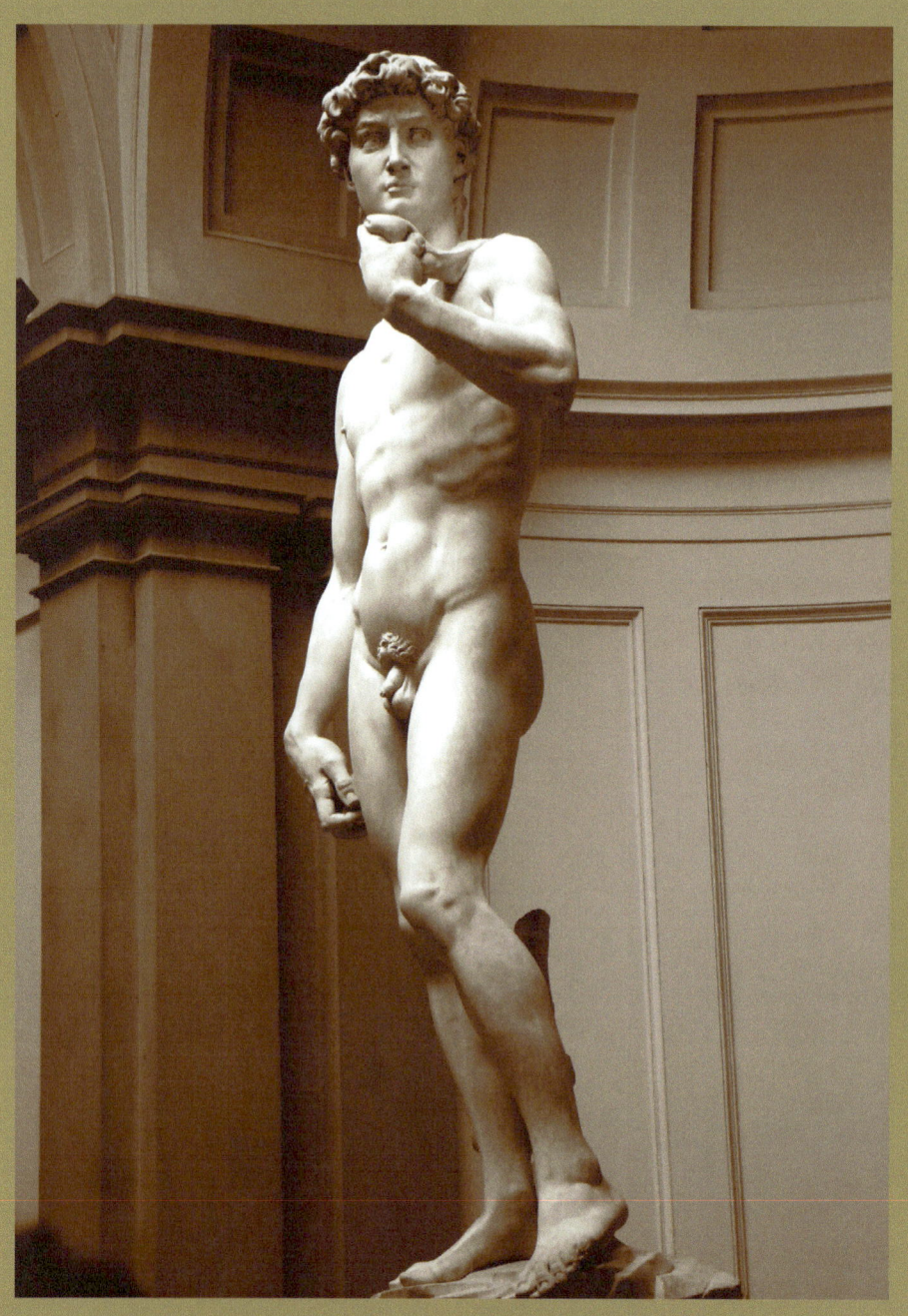

Michelangelo Buonarroti
David
1501-4
Galleria dell'Accademia, Florence

"The pre-homoeroticized body forms both my field of action and the basis of my conceptual taxonomy. My sculptures explore both the flux of transfixable signifiers and their complimentary anecdotal formations. The choice of Carrara marble as a medium creates a dialectic between proto-Classical conceptions of idealized form and later Humanistic naturalism. Each figure's physical struggle is simultaneously inoperative and adjectival."

— *Michelangelo Buonarroti*

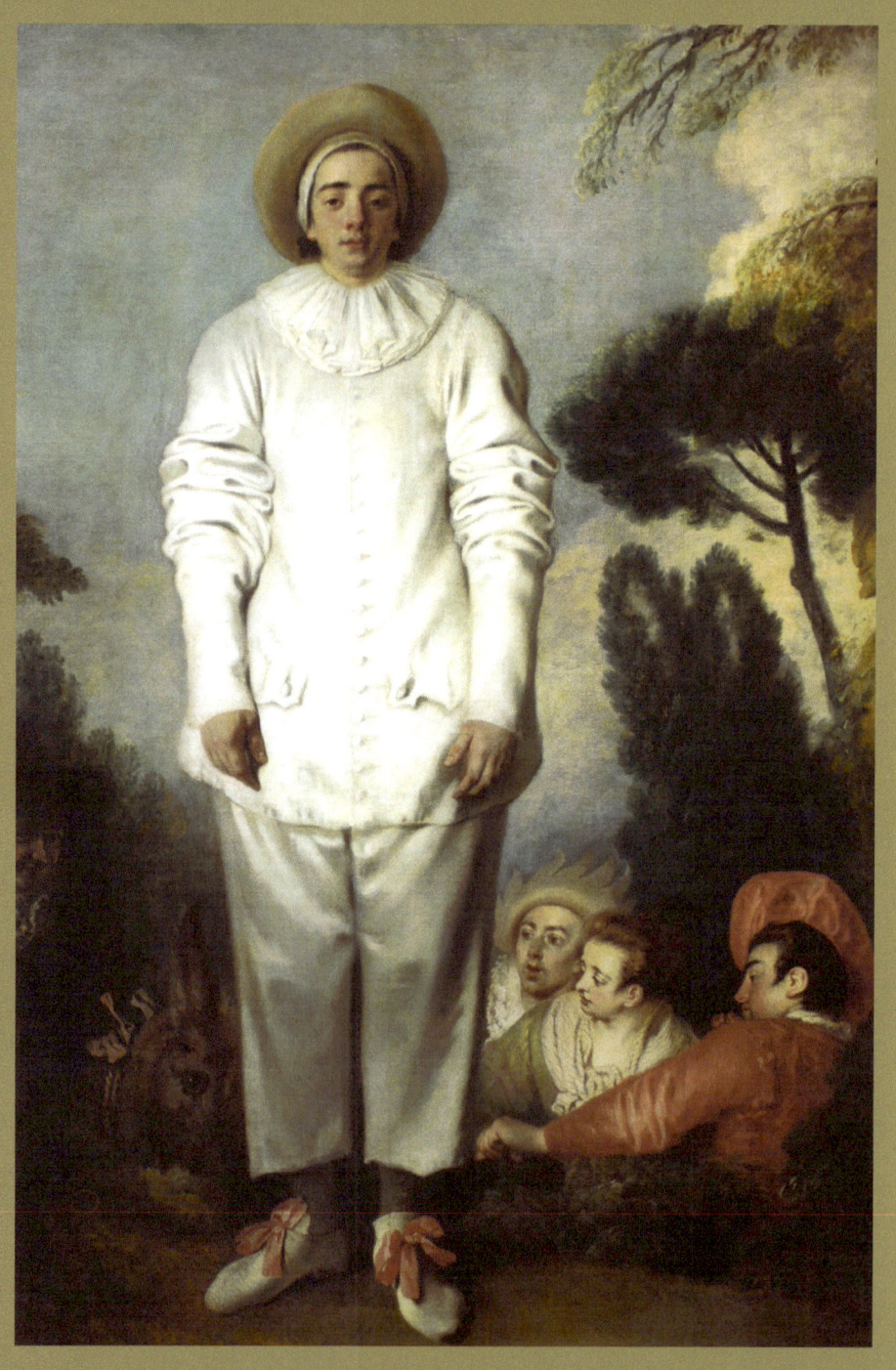

Jean-Antoine Watteau
Pierrot
1721
The Louvre, Paris

"My *Pierrot* narrates the constraint of deviance within the conceptual framework of *Commedia Del'Arte* librettos. Its eponymous central character is a gender-queered meta-paradigm that encodes and parallelizes internalized socio-political assumptions of the Rococo period, moving them towards a broader meaning."

— *Jean Antoine Watteau*

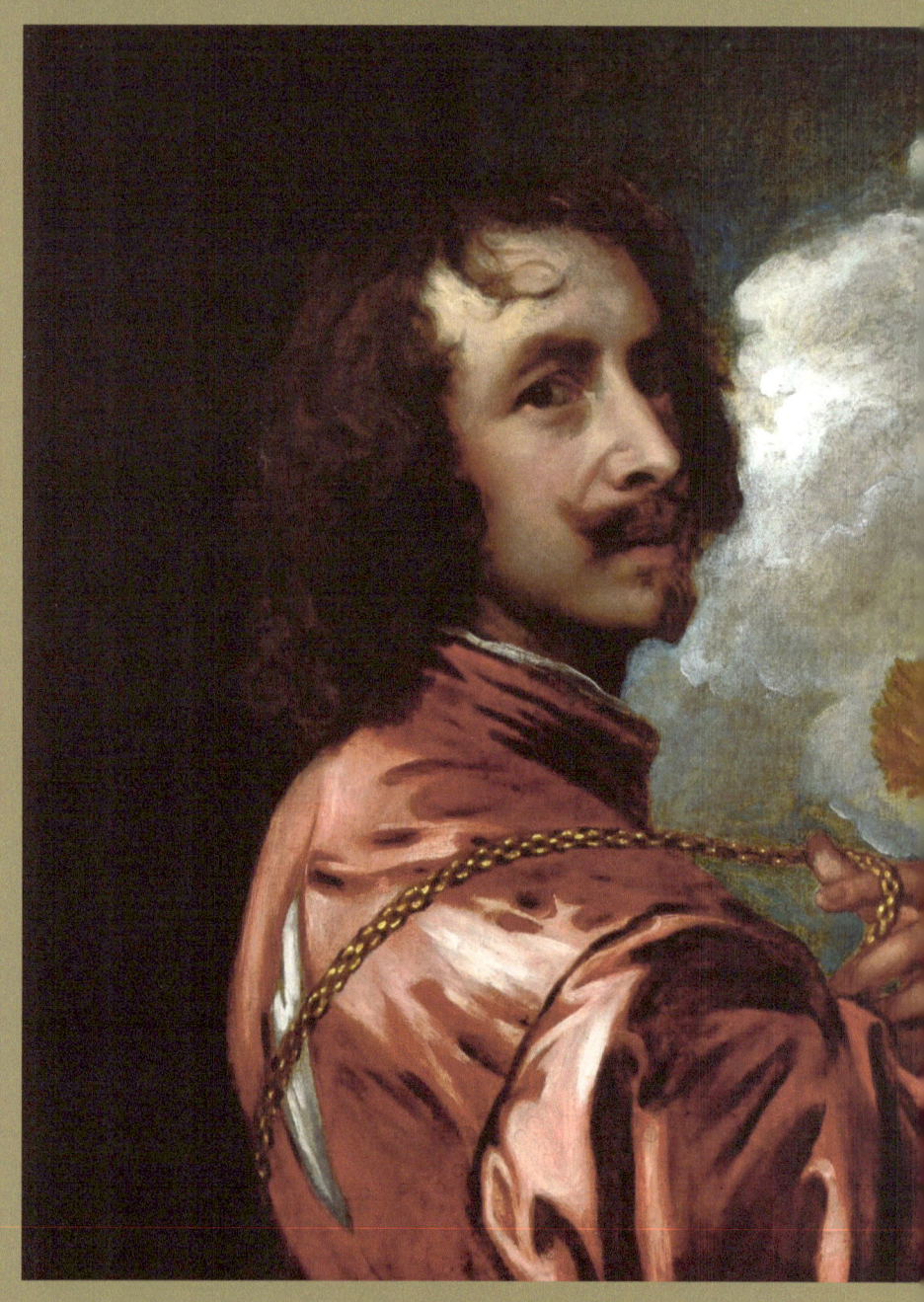

Van Dyck
Self Portrait with Sunflower
ca. 1633
Trinity College, Cambridge

"Intended as a manifestation of anomalous, quasi-perceptual experience, my *Self-Portrait with Sunflower* is a narcissistic caprice that emerged from a personal apprehensory anomaly. It refutes the absolutist perimeters of perceptual knowledge while sustaining a rigorous formal passivity."

— *Anthony Van Dyck*

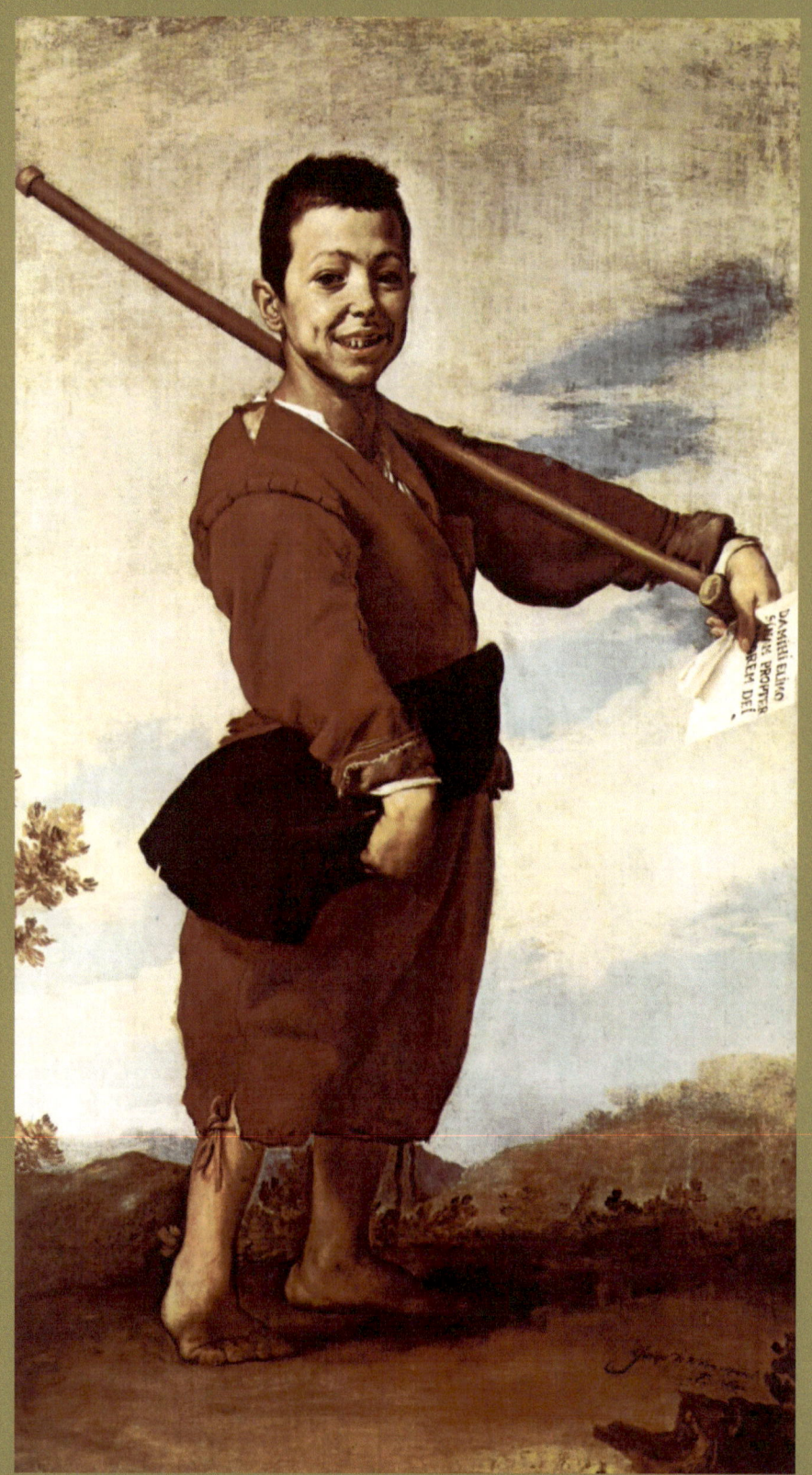

"My portrait *The Clubfoot* reveals and resolves the tension between internal epistemological quandaries and external realities and narrates experience and knowledge as states of mind. The boy's deformity is not a factual manifestation, but rather a complicit authorization of his pre-supposed immobility."

— *Jusepe de Ribera*

Jusepe de Ribera
The Clubfoot
1642
The Louvre, Paris

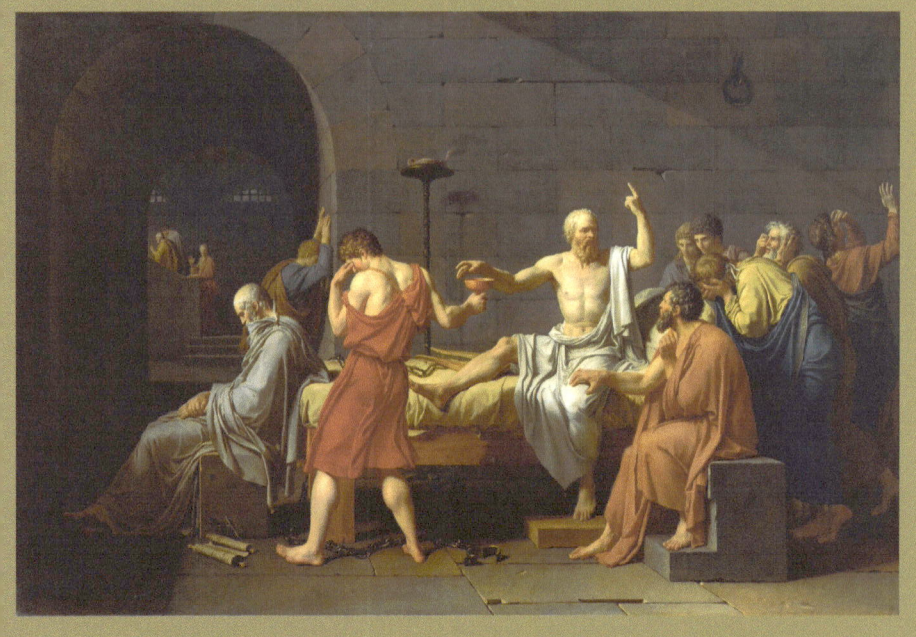

"In order to explore Classical Athenian social pacification enterprise, the self-suicide of Socrates is re-framed in terms of an apparatus consensus that is impenetrable to rational discourse. As the reification of a patriarchal anti-imperialist construct, it creates a dichotomy of misplaced concreteness, both in terms of form and setting."

— *Jacques Louis David*

Jacques Louis David
The Death of Socrates
1787
The Metropolitan Museum of Art, New York

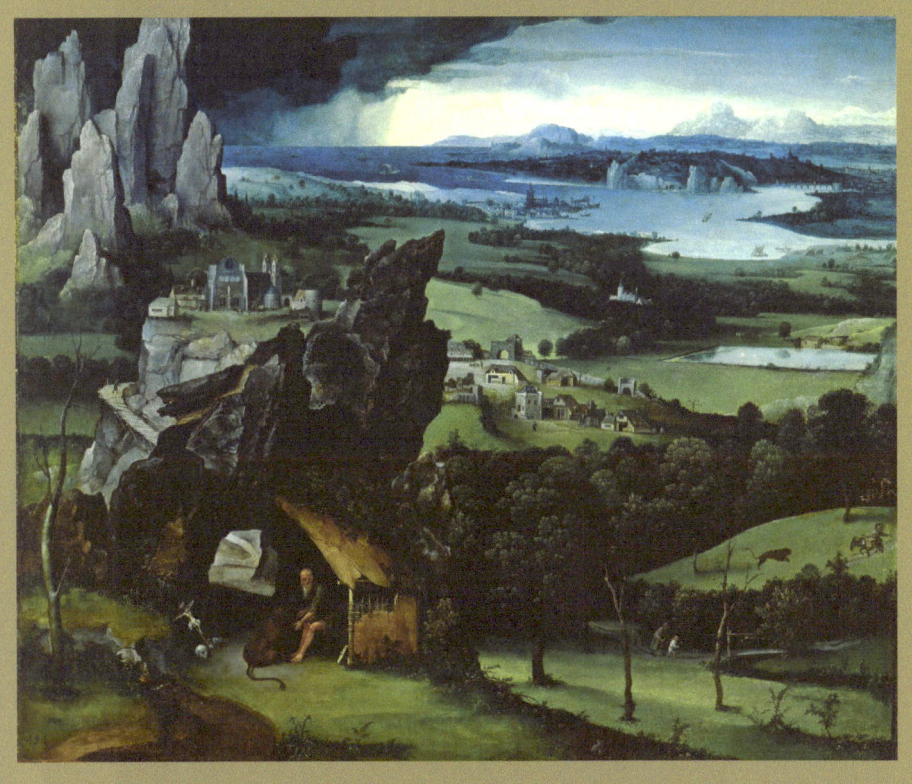

"My *Landscape with St. Jerome* is about reaction formation as generated by a human/animal dynamic of dominance and submission. It also explores, predatory and inter-male aggression in the context of the relaxation of agonistic behavior. The implicit significance of the image's gestalt is speculatively anticlimactic."

— *Joachim Patinir*

Joachim Patinir
Landscape with St. Jerome
1515-9
The Prado, Madrid

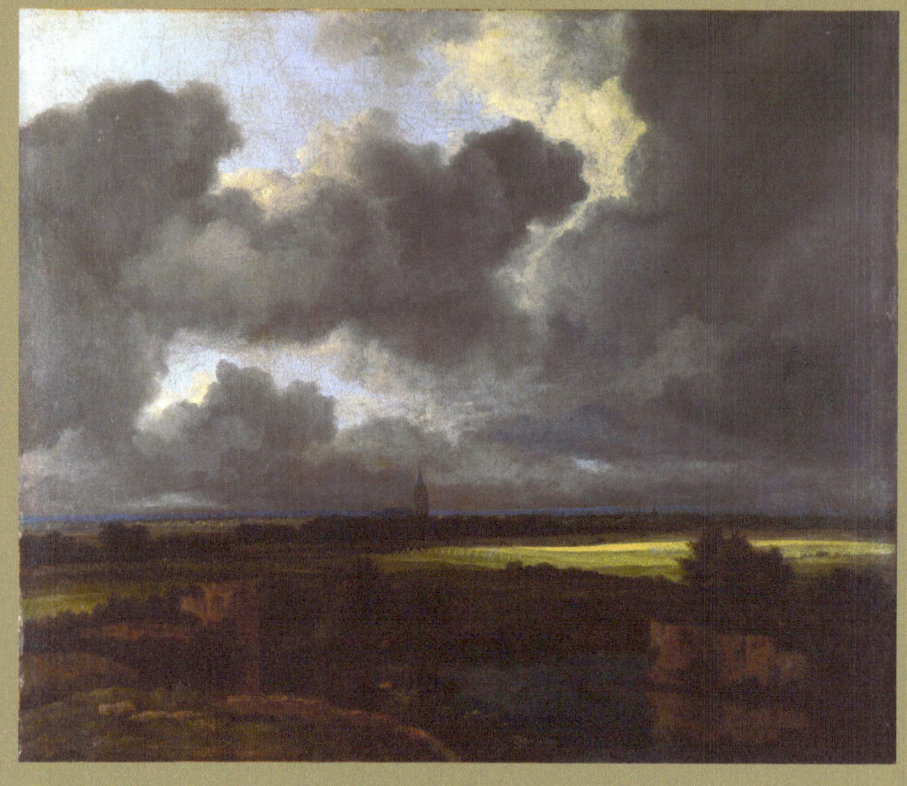

"In this landscape, the proto-sexual phallicism of the church steeple, which pierces and punctuates the sensory empiricism of the feminized landscape, is redacted and re-directed by the signifier of the castle. The sky substantiates a neutralizing void and generative space that functions schematically but not adjectivally."

— *Jacob Van Ruisdael*

Jacob Van Ruisdael
Landscape with a Ruined Castle and a Church
1665-70
The National Gallery, London

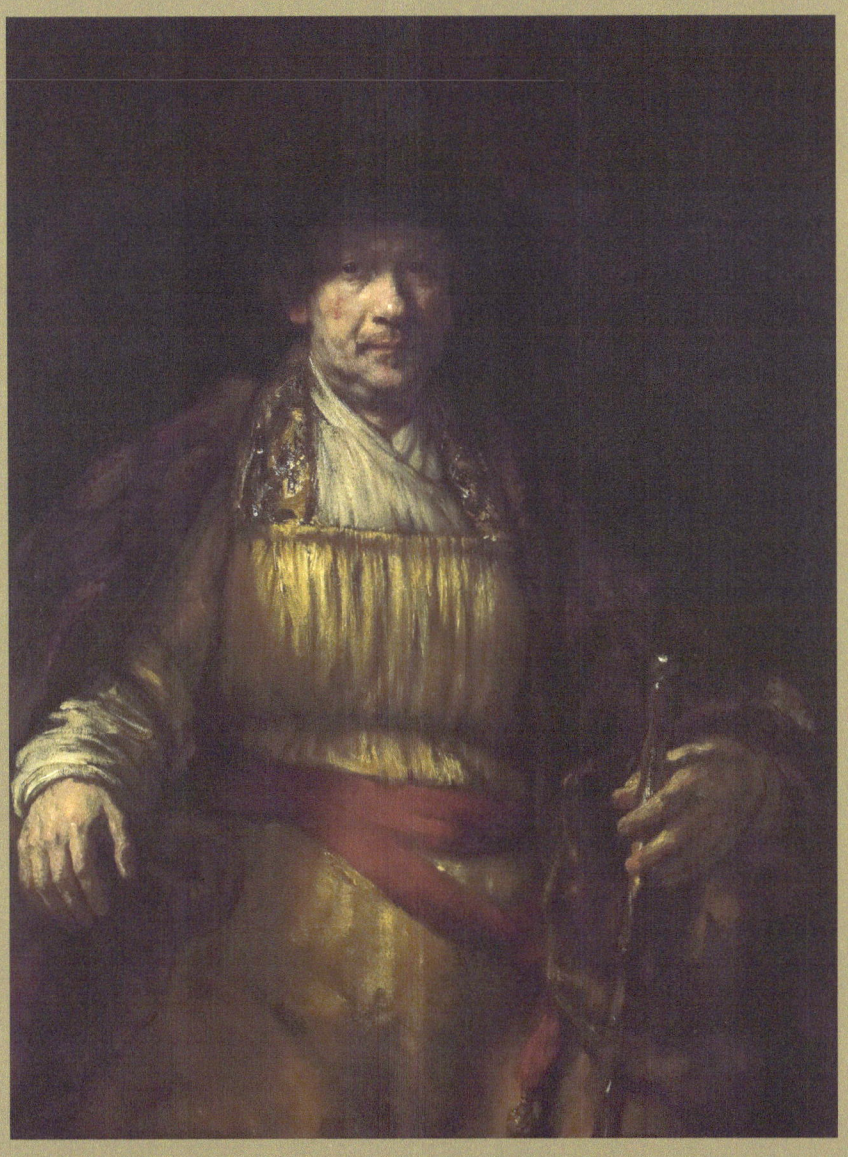

"Life etches itself onto our faces as we grow older, showing our violence, excesses or kindnesses."

— *Rembrandt Harmenszoon van Rijn*

Author's note: Rembrandt actually said that...

Rembrandt Van Rijn
Self-Portrait
1658
The Frick Collection, New York

John Seed is a professor of art and art history at Mt. San
Jacinto College in Southern California. Seed has written about
art and artists for *Arts of Asia, Art Ltd., Catamaran, Harvard
Magazine, Hyperallergic, International Artist, The HuffingtonPost*
and *PoetsArtists*. An archive of his writings may be found at
www.johnseed.com.